And Then There Was Jesus

Pooja Chilukuri

Rain Publishing

KNIGHTDALE, NORTH CAROLINA

Pooja Chilukuri/Rain Publishing, LLC
PO Box 702
Knightdale, NC 27545
www.rainpublishing.com

Cover Design: www.SDCreativeworks.com

Edited by Sherrian Crumbley

Ordering Information:

Quantity sales. Special discounts are available on quantity purchases by corporations, associations, and others. For details, contact the "Special Sales Department" at the address above.

And Then There Was Jesus/ Pooja Chilukuri. – 1st ed.
ISBN 978-0-9962421-6-5

Published and Printed in the United States of America

Dedication

This book is dedicated to my creator, without whom my being could not have been conceived nor my life's journey possible...

Dear Denise
Let your light shine))
always ¨

With love)

Rooja

Acknowledgements

To *Mom and Dad*, thank you for your love, courage, compassion and faith. Your belief in God through good and bad times, inspired my own spiritual journey.

To *Amma and Nanna*, thank you for raising a wonderful human being and gifting him to me. The fruit does not fall far from the tree. I am truly blessed to have such loving parents-in-law.

To my husband *Ravi*, I remain deeply grateful to God for bringing you into my life. I am humbled by your spirit of endurance, for always being calm and composed and for teaching me to stay strong and never give up. Thank you for the patience with which you have stood by my side throughout my spiritual roller coaster. I have much to learn from you yet...

Thank you, *Nidhi and Niyati*. This book could not be completed without the valuable feedback and encouragement that you both provided during my writing journey.

I would also like to thank my editor *Sherrian Crumbley*, my publisher, *Rachel Renee Smith* and her team, for their hard work and guidance. I am also grateful to *Pastor Patrick Jensen*, for his encouragement and support, and *Jimi Clemons* for his timely help and advice.

And finally, heartfelt thanks to all my *family members and friends*, who have been a part of my life's journey and allowed me to be a part of theirs. My soul is enriched by what I have learned from each and every one of you!

But most of all, I would like to thank my savior, *Jesus*. Thank you, *Jesus*, for your sacrifice and for being the most faithful friend any human being could ever hope to have. Without you, I would have no story to tell!

CONTENTS

AND THEN THERE WAS JESUS

ABOUT THE AUTHOR

And Then There Was Jesus

Pooja Chilukuri

INTRODUCTION

This book is the story of a devout Hindu girl, a deeply committed Christian young adult, a woman who developed distrust and disillusionment of God (especially the Christian God) and a woman who fell in love with Jesus. All those people are me. This book is my story.

I was a devout Hindu, a sincere God seeker, a dutiful follower of rituals and traditions and committed to raking up good karma for my next life. A series of miraculous events led me to Christianity. I learned to have a relationship with God independent of rituals and traditions. Constant prayers, following Bible principles and seeking after God's will for my life characterized my Christian life. So far, so good. However, soon the spirit of religion caught up with me. It was disguised as good Christian conduct, self-sacrifice, works of charity, service in the church and the careful observance of every letter in the Bible - as interpreted by church leaders - as a means of gaining God's approval. Needless to say, not only did it not work, it left me damaged within, wounded in my soul and wanting nothing to do with God - especially the Christian God. Thus ended my Christian life. What (or who) followed next, was outside the scope of my wildest imagination. His name is Jesus.

By making my very personal and private spiritual journey public through this book, I want to reach out to all those who have been spiritually damaged, wounded in their soul and disillusioned by God. I believe that there are many today who are disappointed and deeply hurt by the God whom they have served in spiritually toxic religious systems. There are many who experience Christianity as a burden, whose Christian life revolves around excessive sacrifice and service as the primary means of gaining God's approval. If you believe that God is displeased with you at the slightest deviation from what your church or pastor preaches, and you have never been consumed by the overwhelming love of God, this book is for you.

I have recorded my journey as it happened. I have not intended to cause any hurt or damage to anyone's religious sentiments. I write mostly from my experiences with both Hinduism and Christianity - the two religions that have defined my life. This book is my testimony that religion simply does not work. It fails at the very thing it supposedly aims to do: to bring people closer to God. On the contrary, religion successfully drives a wedge between God and man by producing fear and guilt. Religion also aims to bring loving and peace-ful conduct between humans through sacrificial acts of service and good moral conduct. Why then has it been so successful in creating factions, inhuman treatment and judgment of fellow humans? Religion does not give us a transformed heart (the place where desire for evil vanishes), a peaceful conscience and a joyful soul, but Jesus does. Religion always compels us to measure up to God's standards. Jesus compels us to rest in God's love and His finished work on the cross. Jesus brings the hope that religion cannot give, the hope that you do not have to struggle to be approved by God. He is al-ready deeply in love with you.

My prayer is that this book brings both hope and healing.

THERE WAS HINDUISM

"There is a God shaped vacuum in the heart of every man which cannot be filled by any created thing..." –Blaise Pascal

Of Temple Bells

Ding ding ding ding ding ding ding ding.... I woke up to that familiar sound of the temple bell every morning. The sound of the bell was followed by the fragrance of burnt incense sticks. The memory remains etched in my soul - my dad offering his morning prayers to the many gods in our temple at home. The temple bell was like a snooze button on an alarm clock. As soon as I heard it, I knew that there was at least an hour more that I could sleep in. It was in that hour, as I struggled between sleeping and waking, that my dad dutifully offered his morning prayers to Krishna, Hanuman, Shiva and Durga. These were some of the deities whose idols and images were housed in our temple at home. From my bed, I could hear the sound of many chantings: the mantras of Jainism (the way of life established by Mahavira, who was Buddha's contemporary) and the

Hanuman Chalisa mantras (prayers offered to the god Hanuman) followed by the Hare Krishna chantings (prayers offered to the god Krishna). Thus every morn-ing I was introduced to God, a supreme being who could take on many forms and who had many names.

God was someone impossible to avoid. I learned that very early on in my human journey. My very name, Pooja, was a reminder. Pooja means worship. Pooja also refers to rituals that are part of the Hindu worship ceremonies. I was born on the day of Saraswati Pooja, a day set aside to seek the blessings of the goddess Saraswati, in order to receive the gifts of intelligence and good grades in school examinations. I was born in the city of Calcutta, India, where this festival is considered auspicious. This made selecting a name for me very easy. With no second thoughts, my grandfather named me Pooja, a constant reminder that there is a supreme being to whom poojas must be offered. If that was not enough of a reminder, I could not walk a few steps around the block without running into altars that had sprung up overnight. People would claim that they re-ceived a miracle or an answered prayer at a certain spot in the middle of the sidewalk. Then they would place a stone and offer ceremonial flowers to it. Before you knew it, there it was - a temple that emerged overnight. Indeed, there was no arguing faith with reason. Besides these little altars everywhere, there were huge temples all over the city. These housed big and powerful deities.

Each deity provided a different blessing although they were considered part of the same supreme source. My family needed blessings from the god Ganesha before we ventured into anything new and dared not displease the god Shiva for fear of destruction. The god Vishnu, who had several incarnations, including the most pop-ular Ram and Krishna, was much revered in my home along with the goddess Durga. I remember doing extensive rituals to please Durga so she would protect our household from many demons, for she had the com-bined power of the major gods that enabled her to do so. The creator, Brahma, did not get much attention in my home, but he did not seem to be that important, occasionally showing up in some stories that were recited as part of some ceremonies and rituals. My grand-mother had many stories to narrate, one connected to each deity, thereby fueling my belief in God.

Being part of such a religious family, there was no escaping God. God was to be revered and worshipped through rituals. In return, He watched over you and kept evil away. I conducted all the right rituals in their proper manner and focused on doing good karma, in order to avoid collecting punishment for a future birth. I routinely accompanied my family on temple visits. We frequently invited priests to our home to perform rituals to keep evil away. I was well versed in those rituals. Each ritual was supposed to bring a specific blessing, either protection or prosperity. However, I often found them to be monotonous. Frequently, I sat on my win-dow ledge and talked to God at length. I thought that I may be better off telling God my problems rather than repeating the same rituals over and over again. This way, he could help me more specifically than being gen-eral with his blessings. Where rituals were boring for me, religious festivals were full of fun. I participated in all religious festivals at home and in the community. Hinduism had a special place in my life. It was the thread that connected me to my family and friends.

A lot has happened since my childhood days but not enough to erase the sound of the temple bells from my memories. How could I forget? It was my very first introduction to God.

Here a God,
There a God

Hinduism was indeed my cultural and religious identity, but it was not the only religious influence in my life. My family was also inspired by Jainism, Bud-dhism, Islam and Christianity. My mother believed that my brother was born to her as a result of offering prayers to the Muslim saint, Salim Chishti, during her visit to Fatehpur Sikri - a walled city built by the Mughal king Akbar, in the sixteenth century, to honor the Sufi saint. I lived in Calcutta, home to many Muslim communities. The festival of Eid was widely celebrated in the city. India is also the birthplace of Siddharta Gautama or Buddha. We were made well aware of his teachings along with the teachings of Mahavira, the founder of Jainism. My grandfather actually followed the mandates of Jainism strictly and my father did not let a day go by without reciting the Jain mantras. One cannot visit Calcutta and ignore St. Paul's Cathedral. It stands as a towering landmark in a busy part of the city, a reminder that Christianity touched the city at some point in his-tory. Nor can one live in Calcutta and not be touched by the work of Mother Teresa, whose Christian values helped her to embrace the lepers and the poor, those whom society rejected. My dad's best friend, or uncle, as we referred to him, was a Christian. He introduced us to Easter eggs and Bible stories. In the pages of the Bible story book, I was introduced to the Ten Com-mandments and Jesus Christ. As far as the commandments were concerned, I agreed whole heartedly with the Christian God. I did not see how civilization could function without these rules. About Jesus, however, I had the impression that he was a good man, a prophet sent by God and a worker of miracles. All I knew was that he had been crucified by some "wicked" people. After being dead for three days, Jesus came out alive. This then entitled us to candy filled chocolate coated eggs on the occasion Christians referred to as Easter. I loved celebrating all religious festivals because of the food and fun. Christmas and Easter were no exception. Because of our connection to this uncle, we enjoyed both the Christmas tree and the Easter egg.

I identified myself as a Hindu, but as far as my religious practices, I did not limit myself to any one religion. I believed that all gods were simply an expression of the one Supreme Being who created the universe. I believed in good karma and in celebrating all religious festivals with equal enthusiasm. Who can pass up food and fun? I wish that my religious life had re-mained that simple. But alas, it has been rightfully said that change is the only constant. And so it was. Things changed.

three

God God Everywhere But Not One For Me

By the time I was into my teenage years, I was drowning in religious activities. I had integrated all re-ligions into my life and was content for a while. However, soon I became restless. There was something missing. In spite of having the knowledge of diverse religions, and following so many rituals and performing so many worship ceremonies (poojas), I felt empty inside. I was not at peace within myself. There was a vague sense of fear that hung over my family and friends with regard to God - the fear that if anything went wrong in the way the rituals were done or if we slipped up in our karma, something evil would come our way. It seemed like God was difficult to please and no amount of rituals could satisfy him. Religion no longer appeared to be an innocent and happy affair.

Much to my disappointment, I started noticing that all religions were not the same after all. The differences were so great that it led to communal killings. I still remember the day when there was a bomb scare in the heart of the city due to rioting between Hindus and Muslims causing my dad and me to run for shelter. This was followed by a curfew and much tension in the air. This was not the first time that India had experienced these religious riots on such a large scale. My family, also, was no stranger to communal killings. My grand-father had fled the country of Pakistan during the communal killings that followed the partition of India and Pakistan in 1947. He left behind his ancestral home and livelihood. He was not alone. Millions of people, both Hindus and Muslims were displaced during that time and hundreds of thousands were killed. All for religion. Why? If all religions are the same and all gods are expressions of the one God, why were Hindus and Muslims killing each other? Is that who God was - someone who would create so many religious paths to get to Him and then create fighting and killings among humans to promote one religion over another?

And if that was not bad enough, we had the caste system which was promoted by religion itself. Why would any God create these humans and then promote inequality among them for the sake of religion? God,

Himself, appeared to be very confusing. What was He like anyways? Was He on the side of war or on the side of peace? Why did dharma (religious duties) require the god Rama to banish his pregnant wife into exile (Ramayana)? Was it ok to tell a lie for the sake of dharma (Mahabharata) or was the commandment "Thou shall not lie" (Bible) the absolute moral standard? My vision of God was getting blurry and I could no longer make sense of Him. The fact that there was evil and suffering in the world did not help. If God was all powerful then why could He not put an end to all the suffering in this world? I was plagued and bothered by these and many other questions. I felt an emptiness inside. No matter what the religion, God seemed like someone who did what He pleased and very impersonal. It seemed like He cared only about our conduct and our works (karma) and kept a meticulous record of the same.

At first I had wanted to be close to this being who created me but with time, I thought it was best to main-tain my distance from Him. I wanted to get to know God for who He was but found that what I conceived in my heart about Him (that He ought to care for and love what He created) did not match up to how I felt about Him (confused and intimidated). So, for the time being, I did what any teenager may have done. I decided to give up looking for God. There were many gods everywhere, but not one of them was for me. Besides, why worry about God until it's time to meet Him and meeting Him was a long ways away - or was it?

four

"I Don't Want to Die"

And so it happened. I decided to shift my focus from God on to my ambitions. There was a lot to do. A lot to prove. Women in my family, typically, were not encouraged to pursue higher levels of education. They married young into large extended-family households where they served as a wife, mother and dutiful daughter in laws. There were no women scientists or other professionals among my ancestors that I knew of. Thanks to the courage and motivation my parents provided, I sought to create an identity for myself. I wanted to be a doctor, and so I drowned myself in academics. My whole life was ahead of me and I could not waste it worrying about God. I needed to go after my dreams and make my parents proud. I took it upon myself to liberate the other women in my family from being in bondage to the mindset that girls cannot be achievers outside the home. God would have to wait.

God chose not to wait.

Soon after graduating from high school, I gained admission into a prestigious medical college in Calcutta. I was all set to become the very first female doctor in my family. My dreams were on the verge of being fulfilled, when life did what it does best - it sprung a surprise on me. I thought I would be the one to save people's lives. Instead, I found myself struggling to save my own. I fell seriously ill with a condition that could not be diagnosed nor treated. The doctors were confounded and no one around me knew where to start looking for answers to my problem. What was my problem? I started having some very peculiar symptoms. Early in morning, about 3am, I would experience violent back-to-back, non-stop episodes of vomiting. This would continue until about 10 am. Then it would suddenly stop and start all over again the next morning at 3 am. This pattern of severe vomiting continued for more than one year, day after day. I had to be fed with the equivalent of a feeding tube by liquefying all foods and sipping with a spoon. I could hardly get any food in. Soon I became severely dehydrated and drained of every ounce of energy. I was unable to move much, eat or drink. These episodes could not be controlled by any medication. Needless to say, I started wasting away. None of the medical minds around me were able to help. They tried but to no avail.

I remember being on at least seven different medications at a given time. None of them worked. Added to this was a moral and spiritual complication. Was God mad at me? Why had He struck me with such a strange disease? What was this disease? Was this a punishment for not thinking about God anymore? Had I messed up in my karma somewhere? Did I break His rules? I was physically sick, yes, but it was these thoughts of condemnation and fear that led me to depression. There was a sense of impending doom. I was going to die. There was no denying this truth. No one had been able to help me and I was wasting away from not being able to eat or sleep. I cannot imagine the trauma that my parents went through. I remember my parents spend-ing sleepless nights by my side. I would be up all night scared and depressed and staring in the dark, not knowing what tomorrow held.

I heard whispers in passing: "It is a demonic spirit." "It is witchcraft." "Someone has cast an evil eye!" "Is she just going insane?" "Is it all in her mind?" The people around us started spreading all kinds of rumors. This ended up being socially and culturally demoralizing for my family. I had to terminate my medical studies. I could not keep up my attendance. My world fell apart. My dreams were crushed. Why God, why?

When one cannot find answers in the physical realm, one turns to the supernatural. My dad was desperately searching for a cure and when doctors failed, he turned to god, not to one but to many of them. As for me, I had only one thought, "I don't want to die." I was terrified of dying. I was only eighteen.

five

Oh My Gods!

It was before dawn when my dad walked into my room. I was in the middle of an intense vomiting session - a normal affair by this time. He did not bat an eye lid. He had fixed a container near my bed to help me do this comfortably. My heart went out to him. I knew it was hard for him to see me suffer. But my dad was not one to give up. He had made up his mind to seek answers from the supernatural. We would knock on the door of any and every god we knew. Someone had given him the lead to a "holy man" who lived in a far off vil-lage. This person could cast out demons and heal people through supernatural means. We were going to give it a shot. He had come to my room make sure I was ready for the trip. I was ready. I did not care where we went or which god we prayed to or how I got healed. I just knew that I wanted to get better. And so, after a nice, long car ride, we arrived at the hut of this holy man. What I encountered at this place was truly "out of this world". This man believed that I was the victim of a highly specific witchcraft called "arrow witchcraft" where the target is under a spell that causes them to waste away slowly from not being able to eat or function emotionally. He believed that my intestines had been the target of this spell which was cast on me via eating some cursed food. He claimed that this food was still attached to my intestines and that he could remove it non-surgically. I laid down as he "prayed" over me and put an empty bowl on my stomach, over my belly button and walked away leaving me alone in that room with my dad. Soon, I felt a churning in my belly button and a soreness. The next thing I knew, there was goop oozing out of my belly button into that bowl. I could not believe it! What was more unbelievable was that my navel hurt and was tender. It felt like I had a surgery. I did not trust this man. It was clear to me that this man was far from holy and well versed in supernatural powers indeed. This man was far less interested in fixing my problem and far more interested in fixing his retirement plan. I knew this when he could not fix my problem in the first visit and asked that we keep coming back for more. We said goodbye. They say that a drowning man will grasp at a straw and we had no choice but to follow every lead that came our way in the hope that one of them would work. We kept offering several pray-ers to the Hindu gods, calling out to them, chanting their names and doing many religious ceremonies and rituals at home. When all the Hindu gods, rituals and prayers seemingly failed, we turned to the faith of our Muslim friends. It was time to visit the Mazar. A Mazar is a memorial of a holy, Muslim saint. The Mazar in Calcutta was built upon the grave of a Sufi saint. The ground, where the deceased saint was buried, was raised up, covered with a cloth and decorated with flowers. This is where prayers were offered and miracles of faith took place. I do not remember exactly how many days and nights we spent there looking for a miraculous healing, following all the customs and requirements laid out in front of us. One of my friends claimed that she was healed in that place. She had suffered from a chronic physical ailment similar to mine, which she believed was also due to witchcraft. Because I trusted her judgment, I decided to give it my best shot. I decided to apply faith and pray wholeheartedly at this Mazar, but was left feeling exhausted and discouraged when it did not work for me.

Soon after, someone, who claimed to have special "praying powers", was referred to us. After he cleared the "air" from around me, I fell into a deep sleep. I had not slept for months prior to this. It was in this sleep that I had a beautiful dream. I saw a building that closely resembled a church. There were no idols or images inside, only a voice telling me that I was looking for healing in the wrong places. I snapped out of the dream not knowing what it meant. I passed it off as a figment of my imagination. I was happy to have slept for some time. I was disappointed with God but willing to give Him one last try by going on a journey to the shrine of Sai Baba in the town of Shirdia place where hope and faith meet with answered prayers for many. Unfortunately, it sadly left me disappointed and disillusioned without healing and without any hope for my future.

We had tried our best to get help from God with faith and a sincere heart but He seemed to have turned deaf. So we gave up on God and went back to pursuing the medical approach. It was at this time that we met some-one from Duke University, North Carolina (NC), who was visiting India. To make a long story short, before I knew it, I was on my way to Meredith College, NC, USA as an undergraduate student. The plan was to get help at the Duke medical center while residing in the US as a student at Meredith College. This was a desperate shot in the dark. I did not even know if physically my body could handle the journey or the change, but things felt so hopeless that I had nothing to lose by trying. If I died because my body could not handle the stress of the journey, I did not care. I saw no signs of being able to stay alive if I left things status quo. I decided to take the plunge.

In The Land Of The Free

December of 1992 will be hard to forget. I said goodbye to my parents, my family, my friends and my city, not knowing if I would ever see them again. Amidst all the tears and the heaviness of parting with the only people and life that I knew, all I could remember was my parents' helplessness mixed with hope. My uncle, my dad's cousin, was going to accompany me on the long plane ride but I knew that I would be alone. I knew that my mom and dad would no longer be around for me to depend on. It was the dark ages when people depended on aerograms to communicate across the ocean. I had no way of even talking (emails and cell phones were not in vogue yet) to my family everyday once I left India.

Yes, I was going to be on my own. I cannot tell to this day whether it was desperation or faith that led my parents to make that choice. Maybe it was both. They still held on to the belief that there was a God and that He would keep their daughter safe. I just went along with their decision because all other doors to hope remained barred. I had to give this open door a fair try. Would I find a new life in the USA? Would I even be alive? Was I better off dying at home with my family around me? Would I find a cure for my ailment? So many questions went through my head. No one questioned my being sick on the plane; they passed it off for motion sickness. For once, I was not embarrassed by my physical situation. Maybe things would not be so bad after all. When I landed, I was greeted by the Statue of Liberty and by another one of my dad's relatives who lived in New York. I still remember the bitter cold winter, the busyness of New York City, the people rushing along with their businesses, and the subways. Yes, the city was alive and beautiful but I was homesick and filled with uncertainty regarding the days ahead.

I lived in a small apartment in New York City, with my uncle. I stayed there for one week before a long Greyhound bus ride brought me to Meredith College, Raleigh NC, in January 1993. While in New York, I would look out my bedroom window, scrutinizing the city and the people. The whole city was lit and decorated for Christmas not to mention the beautiful churches with large crosses on their steeple, standing tall, reminding me of God again and again. However, it never occurred to me to go inside an actual church or seek healing from the Christian God. I was getting tired of being disappointed with God. Besides, I was looking forward to getting any medical help that I might be able to get, once I landed in NC. As I looked at the steeple of the church from my bedroom window every day, I could not even imagine that one day Christianity would take over my whole life.

THERE WAS
CHRISTIANITY

You must make your choice. Either this man (Jesus) was, and is, the Son of God, or else a madman or something worse. You can shut him up for a fool, you can spit at him and kill him as a demon or you can fall at his feet and call him Lord and God, but let us not come with any patronizing nonsense about his being a great human teacher. He has not left that open to us, he did not intend to. — C.S. Lewis, Mere Christianity

seven

The Name of Jesus

"Do you believe Jesus is the only God"? "No, of course not," I replied in an attempt to help my international friend, at Meredith College, to complete an assignment for her Religion class. Surely many gods were needed to represent different aspects of the one magnanimous Supreme Being. "Jesus was a good moral teacher and a holy man who was blessed by God to per-form miracles, that's all" – with great firmness, I pronounced my verdict. My answer seemed to satisfy my friend and we did not discuss it any further. It was January of 1993 and I was living on campus at Meredith College with other international students who soon be-came like family.

I tried to cover up my health situation, as best as I could, but not for long. I was unable to get in touch with my Dad's contact at Duke University. This shattered my hopes of finding a medical solution to my problem. I was clueless as to where to turn for help next and so I decided to confide in some of my friends on campus. A couple of them suggested that since I had tried everything else but not church, maybe I needed to give that a try as well. At this point I saw no choice. Once again, I had to try whatever came my way. My friends took me to a pastor's house. The pastor just asked me, "Do you believe that Jesus can heal you?" "Sure," I said. Did I really believe it? Honestly speaking, I did not know. I was hoping against hope. Following that moment of prayer, that night, for the first time in almost a year, I slept like a baby. I slept through the whole night and woke up later in the day with no episodes of vomiting. I was shocked and in disbelief. Although I far from en-joyed it, my sickness had become a part of me and it felt a little strange at first to wake up and be okay. I had forgotten what it felt like to sleep, then awake and have a normal day. I was on my guard all day that I may have to run to the bathroom, but those violent vomiting episodes simply vanished. Just like that, Poof. It was the spring of 1993. Soon after, I celebrated my twentieth birthday. It suddenly hit me - Oh my God, I'm going to live!

I was on my way to better health. There was no doubt about that. However, I was confused and fearful of God. I could no longer ignore Him. I had suffered long and hard and then been healed in an instant. I was fearful of His power. I was troubled by oppressive and negative thought patterns about God. There was a chorus that kept playing inside my head. The "voices" were mostly thoughts of guilt, accusations from events related to my life and past (of course), and questions about karma, my afterlife and how to please God so that I do not have to suffer again. Now that I actually had some glimmer of hope that I was going to live, I needed a way to deal with these inner voices and reconstruct my life and make peace with God. The thing that puzzled me the most was the fact that the God of the universe had chosen to answer me only when I called on Jesus. What was it about this man, Jesus, that God should only answer me through Him? Why not the other gods or holy men? I had tried so hard. Who was Jesus really? The question my friend had asked me ear-lier in the year, "Do you think that Jesus is the only God?" came back to haunt me. I had put off looking for God once before but this life changing experience was enough to make me determined to look for answers and be at peace within, once and for all, where God was concerned. I decided to learn all that I could from the pastor and his wife. I trusted them for their high moral standards as well. They lived out their religion and had committed their lives to serving God. Who could be better teachers for me? They had far more experience with God than I ever did. I finally had people to show me the way. The pastor and his wife took me in as their own daughter. What followed was hours and hours of time spent together where they shared the Bible with me. In the effort to help me deal with the "voices" in my head, they taught me the Christian scriptures and how to pray. Nothing made perfect sense to me, at that time, but I kept coming back for more because it filled my heart with a sense of peace. What began was not only a journey of learning about God, Jesus and Bible, but also a journey of engaging in friendships and relationships with the church leaders and the members of their congregation as well.

While I was on this learning curve, God continued to reveal the power of Jesus' name to me, although I had still not grasped the concept of Jesus' incarnation or divinity. To me He was still a holy man. There is a quote from the Bible, "At the name of Jesus, every knee shall bow and every tongue confess that Jesus Christ is Lord" (Phil.2:11). At first, the lordship of Jesus had no significance in my life, but I was soon going to get a taste of what it may possibly mean for my life, through a number of events that followed. I will narrate one such incident here - the brave of heart read on - all others please skip to the next chapter.

I was alone in my dormitory room and had dozed off with the lights on. I was awakened by what can be best described as a "presence". There were dark shadows in front of me, clearly seen in the light. I was somewhere between sleep and awake, mostly awake but groggy. All of a sudden two "hand–like" things went for my throat.

It is very hard to describe these. They were not real tangible, physical hands. They can be best described as ethereal, but they choked me with a really tangible, physical force. I felt overcome by fear. This was not an experience I was expecting to have. No, I had not seen any horror movies that day and this most certainly was not my imagination. Twenty years later, I still shudder at the thought of it. Just when I thought I was going to breathe my last, I remembered something the pastor had taught me. He had encouraged me several times to pray out loud, the name and blood of Jesus, over myself.

I had no idea what that meant and that night I could not even pray that out loud due to the obvious fact that I was being choked. But in my mind as loud as I could I said, "Jesus, Jesus, Jesus, Jesus...." And before I knew it I was saying the name of Jesus out loud. The thing, whatever it was, had left. This incident etched in my mind, the power of Jesus' name. However, it would be awhile before I would truly let that sink into my heart.

eight

God Speaks

At first, after my healing experience, my religious life was a roller coaster. I prayed with the pastor to "invite Jesus in my heart" and I started going to church faithfully every Sunday and also participated in any Hindu rituals and practices as, and when, I desired. I prayed to Jesus every day and every night I would chant prayers to the god Hanuman using the prayer book - the Hanuman Chalisa. These chantings were meant to ward off evil spirits. Of course, the name of Jesus could do that too, but what if Jesus was off duty some night? Might I need Hanuman to step in? Perhaps it was just habit. After all, it has been said, "old habits die hard".

One night while I was reading the Hanuman Chalisa, I heard a voice. It was sweet and gentle and not like any human voice at all. It may be best described as a "spirit" voice. I cannot tell if it came from within or without but it was clear enough to have my attention. I cannot remember (bear with me, it was twenty years ago) the exact words but I remember thinking that this voice was convicting me that I had no business depending on the Hanuman Chalisa after tasting the power of Jesus over evil. It was not just my conscience. I was used to my conscience torturing me. This voice was something else, something more. This voice was pricking my heart but was sweet and peaceful. I instinctively picked up the Bible and randomly opened it to the gospel of John Chapter 10. I was stunned at the printed words before my eyes. They were the words of Jesus, saying, "He calls his own sheep by name and leads them out. When he has brought out all his own, he goes on ahead of them, and his sheep follow him because they know his voice. But they will never follow a stranger; in fact, they will run away from him because they do not recognize a stranger's voice." My sheep listen to my voice; I know them, and they follow me. I give them eternal life, and they shall never perish; no one will snatch them out of my hand." My eyes were glued to this excerpt. Something magical happened to me in that moment. I knew deep within that Jesus was beckoning me to "follow Him" exclusively. No other gods. No other means to god. Just Jesus. I knew that beyond any shadow of a doubt that it was His "voice" that I had heard and that He did not intend for me to follow "a stranger's voice", meaning that I needed to sever my ties to other gods, goddesses and ritualistic practices. In the days that followed, I started searching the Bible on my own instead of depending solely on the pastor to teach me. I didn't know what it was that I was looking for. Maybe more of Jesus? My convictions of Jesus' incarnation got stronger every day. The evidence was all over the place. His claims: "I am the way", "No one comes to the Father except through me," (John 14:6), "He who believes in me shall never taste death" (John 11:26), "I am the light of this world" (John 6:12), among many other accounts of His life, baffled me. For instance, in spite of tremendous opposition and threat from the Pharisees (the Jewish religious authority in Jesus' day and time), who viewed Jesus as a blasphemer, Jesus continued to heal, work miracles and claim that He and God were one and the same. Jesus had to be delusional for claiming divinity when He knew fully well that such blasphemy was punishable by death under Jewish law. Or was He telling the truth? I had tasted His healing power and power over the spirit world. I had heard His voice. He was no liar. There was only one explanation in my mind-Jesus was God and the only way to get to the one Supreme Being whom I had been looking for all my life. I wanted to follow His ways exclusively. I decided to give up all other religious practices and devote myself to learning more about Jesus. My heart had changed. I believed in Jesus and wanted to identify myself as a Christian. There was only one problem. My choosing Christianity, exclusively, would have social and cultural implications for my family. Did they care? They were too busy feeling relieved that the daughter they never hoped to see again, was alive, healthy and at peace. And so I took the second big plunge in my life (the first one, of course, was when I left India) and in September, 1994, I got baptized.

I became a Christian.

nine

God of Wonders

Thus began my Christian journey. I was greeted by new ideas and concepts as it related to God. I learned that Jesus died to forgive me for my sins which meant salvation for my soul. I welcomed the thought. Finally no more reincarnation to pay for the "sins" of this life but an eternal rest to look forward to. I was taught that connecting with God meant praying daily, seeking His will and guidance and serving Him in and through church activities, which also included serving the community at large. I welcomed these new ideas. They seemed so simple. Besides, for the first time in my life, it felt like my prayers were being heard and there was actually a response from the other side – from God's side.

A series of incidents left me in awe of this God. College students run out of money pretty quickly. I was no exception. I really wanted to pursue my education in the US. I had found a new life, new friends and a new God.

I did not want to cut it short and return to India. I kept praying for funds and to my surprise, someone stepped forward and said that God had impressed upon them to pay my college tuition, more than 90% of it. This was more than what I hoped for. Finally, I had a God who was listening to my prayers and responding. One time, I prayed for a new pair of shoes and that week someone left new shoes for me outside my room. I had not mentioned this need to anyone. Only God knew. Another time, I needed to buy a toothbrush and a friend gave me her stash from her dental visit that same day. One more time, I ran out of money to buy dinner and was going to bed hungry, when there was a knock on my door. It was my hostel mate. "Can you use this?" she asked, holding a bag full of restaurant food to my face. Could I? You cannot imagine how grateful I felt to this God. He was indeed a wonderworking God to me.

Building a connection, a relationship with God, was not the only aspect of my newfound Christian life. Learning about God, entering into many family ties with the people in the church community and serving Jesus by serving in that church community, was the other aspect – an aspect that would eventually go out of control.

ten

"Heigh-Ho," To Church I Go

Church was a very integral part of my Christian life. In fact, it became my life. Let me start from the beginning.

I was healed by Jesus, tasted the power of His name, heard His voice and experienced miraculous responses to simple prayers. It is no wonder that I was filled with passion and zeal for wanting to know all about Jesus and the Bible. My upbringing taught me that I must learn from those who were older, wiser and leaders in their field of expertise. What better person to be my guru than the pastor who helped me? I trusted him completely as he was a morally upright man and very devoted to the God of the Bible and sincerely devoted to helping people. Besides, how could I sit still and not do something in return for the kindness and goodness that

I received from both God and the church people, especially the pastor and his wife? They took me under their wings and taught me all that they could.

For me, true service to God was in serving the church people and serving the priest, or guru, or the "man of God". I felt love and gratitude, both to Jesus and those who helped me learn about Him, so I immersed myself serving the church needs. Whether rain or shine, I was there at church. I taught Sunday school, Vacation Bible School, participated in Bible studies and prayer meetings – some as early as 5:30 am in the morning. Whether it was the women's fellowship or a yard sale, choir practice or Sunday worship - I was there.

When I first joined the church, we were a very small group and resource - limited in terms of actual head count. Whenever there was a need, I took it upon myself to meet it because I cared deeply about the church's needs, equating them to God's desires for my life. Jesus, the church and the pastor were all fused together as one entity in my mind; and not only in my mind alone, this belief was held by many in the congregation and ex-pressed in different ways. For example, people would not make any decision that was not prayed over and blessed by the pastor. If they did not have the pastor's approval, they did not accept it as God's will. There were some who chose to make their own decisions, even if the pastor did not agree with them, and this was put in the bucket of God's "permissive will" as opposed to God's "perfect will" for their life. I wanted to fulfill God's "perfect will" for my life so I started including the pastor and members of the congregation in my every prayer need.

I did not have the experience with God that the el-ders and leaders in my church did. Yes, I had tasted God in special ways but as far as knowing His ways and how to relate with Him, I felt it was best to trust those who had gone before me. I was clueless about my new religion and I was with a group of people who had more than a clue, they had experience in addition to having high moral standards and the attitude of selfless service. I trusted them. Attendance of Sunday services, Church Bible studies and group prayers was considered imperative as the means to please God and grow spiritually. No one was exempt from these spiritual disciplines except for those sick or traveling. I was care-ful never to miss any of these activities. Some semesters I had 21 credit hours of course work to deal with, but it did not put a dent on my church attendance. The more I did, the more was expected out of me and soon I was elevated to the title of "most committed" Christian. This only motivated me to do more. I could not say no as I could not disappoint the very people who helped save my life. Nor could I disappoint the God who saved my life. The more I did in the church, the more credit I was given for my faith. The equation was simple: more faith = more work. I was continuously praised for my courage (changing from a different religion is no easy task) and commitment. I was loved, respected and declared an exemplary Christian. This verdict came from experienced Christians whom I trusted and who shaped my understanding of Christianity. This assured me that I was on the right path.

This was also the time in my life that I developed in-timate and close friendships with people who were more than family. As the church grew, so did my social life. The support system I had in the church kept me from missing my family, my country and my home. Church was also about learning the Bible. I became so well-versed in the Bible that I could recite any verse off the top of my head. There were scriptures and mindsets about God that were hard to understand, and sometimes quite confusing, but I pushed those under the rug. I was secure in my own works as a means of being right with God and careful not to deviate from anything taught in church. These teachings included serving Jesus with "time, talent and treasures", attending church activities faithfully and obeying the church leaders who were helping us build our Christian character, much like a parent. I did all I was taught to do, out of a sense of gratitude and the desire to please God. Besides, my connection to the church secured my connection to God - or so I thought.

eleven

What God Has Joined Together

While my church life flourished, so did my academic life. I graduated from Meredith College, NC with a triple major and a BS degree. I was all set for graduate school. I cannot describe the sense of satisfaction I felt. It was my dream to pursue higher education and it was going to come true. I had been granted admission into North Carolina State University and a MS degree was only two years away.

Heavy involvement in church activities, the academic burden at school and my responsibilities as a laboratory assistant to my professor, left me with no time to date. But some things are meant to be. I met my husband in a Statistics class that we both attended in the very last semester of my graduate school. He did not care for any God or religion. I did. He was from the South (of India); I was from the North (of India).

Opposites attract. A friendship blossomed. Enough said.

Now I had been taught to make every decision by prayer and consulting my pastor and other friends in the church. Their unanimous response to my choice for a husband was, "You cannot think about marrying a non-believer, it does not work." So, I decided to back away from the friendship, temporarily at least. I prayed my heart out. This is something I had not done in a while. Without realizing it, I had stopped looking inward, exchanged the voice of God for the voice of the church leaders and church bible study for my personal meditation time. My prayer time was also deferred to my group prayer meetings at church. However, this crossroads in my life forced me to seek God for myself and ask for a sign. My effort was not without results. I had met my husband an atheist and two years later I married him as a person of faith in Jesus. His journey from atheism to belief deserves his voice, not mine, so I will go on with my story here. Maybe, he will tell his story someday. His change of heart was nothing short of the miraculous sign that I was looking for. God had shown His hand of sovereignty once again in my life.

The decision to marry my husband was a key turning point in my faith. It was the first time since becoming a Christian that I had depended solely on God for making a decision even when, at first, my church family did not approve of it. In spite of their well-in-tended warnings, I had a deep sense of conviction that my friend was indeed the one that God had chosen for me to marry. There was a clear instance where I felt a gentle, sweet voice bringing alive to me the scriptures from Isaiah 53, "A bruised reed he (Jesus) will not break, a smoldering wick he (Jesus) will not snuff out." It would be ten years before I would understand the sig-nificance of this verse for my husband's life. Back then I just took it to mean that God was going to somehow bring this person to faith in Himself someday and He did.

This incident gave me the confidence to connect with God in my own unique way without having to depend on the church group or the pastor whenever a decision was at hand. Sadly, this confidence was short-lived.

twelve

A Happy Family

My family and my husband's family both flew down from India to witness the very first Christian wedding in their respective families. The fact that ours was not an arranged marriage, and that it spanned two opposite cultures (across two different states in India), was not controversial enough. We added a "scandalous" Christian wedding to the already complicated situation.

My church family put together a very beautiful wedding for us. They showered us with wedding flowers, wedding cake, every single item from my gift registry and above all, their love and prayers. I felt blessed to be a part of such a warm and caring community. I was grateful and decided to serve with even more zeal within this church family.

My husband's Christian experience had been very different from mine. Our relationship had been long-distance for the most part, and he did not have a church family like I did. His understanding of God had been shaped by hours of private Bible study whereas mine was primarily shaped by the sermons I heard and the testimonies of people at my church. When he moved to North Carolina, after the wedding, he was happy to join my church for he valued the relationships and friendships that existed in this church group. So we continued to serve, now together, instead of me, alone. The very first week that he moved to North Carolina, following our wedding, we were involved in Vacation Bible School, choir and Sunday school. It was after all for a good cause and a means to also express gratitude for all we had received. I could not let my marriage get in the way of my church duties. I felt responsible for continuing to contribute to all the different church ministries that I was involved in. My husband also served diligently in the church as a deacon and later the treasurer as well. The more we did, the more was expected from us, and the more we were loved and praised and appreciated and used as examples of spiritually committed Christians. Our love for Jesus (measured purely by our service and zeal) was praised. This continued for ten years and two beautiful children, a girl and a boy, were born to us, in spite of life threatening complications for myself, which made it seem like I could never be a mother. The support and care which I received from the people at church and the countless prayers that got me through that time, made me thank God for them everyday. We were in close touch with at least twenty families in the church whom we could count on for prayer and support. That was my whole world in the US. Both my children grew up within a community of people who served and loved God selflessly. What more could I ask from God? He had joined me to my best friend and together we were joined to this body of a believing, caring community. Our children were safe and rooted there as well. All that I left behind in India: my mom dad, siblings, friends, I found in this community of morally upright and caring people who specially rallied together in a time of need. It was one big happy family. How could something this good go wrong?

thirteen

A (Not So) Picture Perfect Life

I had a good life. I had good relationships with everyone in my church community and all the people loved me and my husband. My children were rooted and happy in the church family also. I had a good life with a man who was (and is) an excellent husband and father. My professional life was very satisfying as well. In other words, I had a picture perfect life. Can anything on earth be perfect?

As time went by, I started sensing strong undercurrents in my church - undercurrents of fear, guilt and control. With sleepless nights from having our first baby, the pressures of a job where my husband was on call 24x7 and I had a pager (remember those?) as well, we were barely able to keep up with our involvement in the church. However, we were encouraged to keep up with our commitments. We were told that God would be very pleased with us and bless us. These were people whose view of God I trusted. Besides, stepping down from ministry was equated to letting God down. Bible verses, in fact some of Jesus' parables about use of talents, were used to validate this mindset. Later, I would understand Jesus' words differently, but for that time, it felt like God would be very pleased with my husband's and my commitment to church work. Besides, who can argue against doing God's work? Who can also argue with the natural laws that govern the human body? The stress from our jobs, first time parenting and church responsibilities all at once came crashing down on our physical health. It was not long before my husband developed autoimmune arthritis and I developed a condition similar to asthma, known as RAD.

There were two schools of thought in my church family regarding our health issues. One was the belief that the devil was attacking us to prevent us from doing ministry because we're committed to God. We were deemed brave to be so committed to ministry and we were cheered on. Another line of thought was that the sickness resulted from sin in our life. Either way the solution was not to cut back on what we were doing. A church member, who had actually played a huge part in shaping my faith, had already warned us once that shrinking back from commitments in the church could cause us to incur God's punishment. Thankfully, I did not believe them right away but all of a sudden I was very aware of the very negative opinion prevalent in my church about God.

The underlying sense of fear of God included the image of a God who demands discipline and holiness at all costs. Missing a prayer gathering or being late for church was considered equal to betraying Jesus. There was a family at church that could not keep up with attending all the activities. Later on, when one of their children had some problem, it was believed that it was the result of the family not being spiritually committed (as reflected by their dwindling attendance). Again, this did not make any sense to me because I knew this family well and I knew the logical reason for their problem, which also got resolved in due time. There were more of these incidents where whenever something would go wrong with people who were not "following Bible ways", it was presented as God's displeasure with them.

I was very close to all the leaders within the church, especially to the pastor and his wife. They were like surrogate parents to me. Their opinion about God, church and life mattered to me. My whole Christian journey had started with that first prayer they prayed over me, in their home, during my freshman year at college. I felt like I owed it to them to be an obedient daughter and not to create any conflict when I did not agree with prevailing mindsets and views of God in the group. Yet there was always a nagging feeling deep down in my heart that something was not right. The voice I had heard at times in my life, especially at the beginning of my Christian life, did not seem to belong to a God who could be as harsh as how I now viewed Him to be. Whatever conflict I felt between my view of God and that of the leadership, I pushed it under the rug. No good would come out of trying to explain myself. I learned this from what happened to a friend of mine. My friend was a guitar player in the choir. Because he dared to suggest that the choir play some new contemporary worship music, instead of the same style of music the church was used to, it was perceived as an attack on the music ministry. This person was not unreasonable or quarrelsome. He was only expressing an opinion. I knew then that expressing an opinion which was in direct conflict to the church leaders' ways of doing things (which definitely included their interpretation of the Bible and who God was) was not an option for me. There was another prevailing mindset: one could expect God's full wrath if one hurt or attacked the "man of God" or his ministry. Except that "attack" could also mean a strong difference in opinion. Moreover, I did not want to lose my relationship with the church leaders and their families, being emotionally and spiritually connected to them since my very first days in the US. Therefore I chose the easy way out. The way of denial.

Indeed my life was not picture perfect. It was far from it.

fourteen

Losing My Way

As time went by, I lost some close friends from the group because they chose to move on. They were construed as being misguided and manipulated by the devil and therefore a threat to the ministry, especially to the church unity. I did not believe these people meant any harm but I was confused by the pastor's genuine concern for the situation. He was truly concerned that these people were misguided and he felt parental instincts of grief at them "going astray" as well as a "shepherd's instincts" to protect the church from them. Any conflict I felt in my heart regarding this, I swept under the rug of denial.

In addition to this, it was a very important part of my church culture for people to discuss their life decisions with the church leadership and pray in small groups about it in order to seek after God's will for their lives. Jesus' words, "Thy will be done", was taken very seriously. Those who chose not to include the pastor in their decision-making process were nonspiritual. I really wanted to make sure that I was doing God's perfect will. I did not want to be in God's permissive will because of the implication that I might somehow lose His favor and protection. So I was careful to include the pas-tor and the people in all of my decision making and prayers for the same.

Apart from just praying with the pastor, obeying him was very important. The pastor's spiritual authority was considered equal to the prophets in the Old Testament scriptures. The story of King Saul, who constantly ignored Prophet Samuel's instructions and undermined his authority, was often mentioned during sermons or in small group Bible Study. I did not want to run the risk of having a rebellious attitude. "Obedience (to God) is better than sacrifice" (1 Samuel 15:22) was a scripture often quoted in my church. However, the difference be-tween obeying the pastor and obeying God was not very clear. This was not a problem because I trusted the pas-tor's counsel and judgment.

I observed how carefully he followed the principles in the Bible and was impressed by his moral integrity and commitment to God and his heart for serving people. Besides, he genuinely cared about my spiritual wellbeing and felt responsible for my spiritual growth, so I decided to be the most obedient Christian ever. I lived under the illusion that my life was very pleasing to God. That was the most dangerous denial of all.

In fact, I had lost my way. I just did not know it yet.

fifteen

A Broken Cistern

Slowly and surely I had lost my way unawares. I was aware only of my responsibilities as a follower of Jesus. I had been taught to take my discipleship to Jesus ("deny myself, carry my cross and follow") very seriously. I even started judging my own spirituality by my performance. The day I did not want to go to church, even if I was genuinely tired, I considered myself to be a bad Christian. Listening to sermons where being fifteen minutes late for church was equal to disappointing Jesus, only added to my shame game. All church related things became Gods perfect will for me. If it was an in-vitation for dinner at a co-worker versus a church activity, I felt obligated to be at the church activity.

Several of Jesus' words were quoted often regarding the cost of being a disciple and how following Jesus meant putting ourselves and our needs last. Taken out of their original context, Jesus' words can be seriously distorted. I did not realize it then. The word joy was defined as Jesus first, Other people next, and You last. But living like this did not bring me the joy it was supposed to. This lack of joy only made me chide myself for a having a bad, ungrateful attitude.

No matter how much I did to please Jesus, he was hard to please, there was always more to do, more of His words, in the Bible, to contend and grapple with. At every Bible study we got to hear at least once that on judgment day God will ask, "What have you done for me?" I was worried that I had not done enough. Additionally, I had my personal holiness to worry about. Asking God to forgive our sins was an important part of our daily cleansing. It was the true Christian act of humility before God to confess and receive forgiveness before we even pray to God, lest our prayers are hindered. So naturally I was always worried about my sins. Going to church felt like a burden. Any guilt or burden we felt was deemed to be God convicting our hearts. No, I did not enjoy church anymore but I felt ashamed of myself for it.

What was wrong with me? Did I not love God anymore? I felt very empty inside and without any peace. I had succeeded in making an idol out of the pastor and the church ministry. I just did not know it yet. In the Bible, God expressed his sorrow for the fact that His people had "forsaken him (God) who is the spring of living water and had dug for themselves broken cisterns that cannot hold water" (Jeremiah 2:13). Indeed my Christian religion was that "broken cistern".

No matter how much I filled up I was always running on empty.

sixteen

God, God, Where Art Thou?

My spirit was asleep. Yes. Was I happy? No. In fact, I felt depressed, disillusioned and disappointed. I had held the belief, even as a child, that finding God would help me to find peace and rest for my heart and soul. The Hindu rituals did not bring me that peace. In fact, I felt threatened by the negative fears and ideas of God that my friends and family seemed to have. The Hindu gods had seemed impossible to please. I gave up on looking for God. When Jesus healed me, I felt a sense of relief. When I heard his "voice", I was ecstatic. At last I had found God. I was only nineteen and had a place for my soul to rest. No more rituals. No more worries about pleasing God. How sweet that salvation message was to me. I was overjoyed at finally having God for a friend, someone whom I could cast my heart and soul upon and who showed me His wonder after wonder – not to men-tion the promise of eternal rest in heaven. Fast forward to the year 2009. I was tired of God. Very discouraged by Jesus' demands and standards, very afraid of the "Father in heaven" who was ready to punish at the slightest deviation and impossible to please. As a Hindu I worried about God punishing me in my next birth. As a Christian I experienced a far worse fear. The punishment would come in this life and would appear as intense tri-als and testing to cleanse me of my "sins". I never knew when God's chastisement was around the corner. Something had gone wrong – terribly, terribly wrong.

My childhood hope of finding God and finding him to be caring and kind was shattered. I had found God, of that I was sure. That I could make him my friend and confidant, I doubted. There were no other gods to fall back on. This was it.
This was God. Take it or leave it.

I wanted desperately to leave it - leave God that is. Once I had decided to give up looking for God and almost died. This time I would run a greater risk, the loss of my salvation, the threat of losing my place with Jesus in Heaven. Not being faithful until the end of our lives, could have serious consequences. I really did not want to have anything to do with God but fear kept me going to church. Fear was not the only emotion I felt. In spite of everything, there was a deep longing for God within my heart, which I could not shake off. I missed feeling that sense of freedom with God that I had first experienced in my early days as a Christian. But where was God? All I experienced was deafening silence on His end, more failing health for both my husband and I and a loss of direction. My family life was falling apart, and my health was falling apart. Constant hives and reactive airways kept me from being productive at both home and work. I eventually had to resign from the job I loved so much and my children always saw a stressed out mom. They were 1 and 5 at this time. They deserved better. I was not able to deliver. I was dried up and miserable, longing for God, only to find Him distant and disapproving. It seemed like it was 1991 all over again where I was sick and crying out to God for healing and guidance but without any hope or any answer. No matter how hard I tried, deafening silence was all I got.

Where was God? Where???

seventeen

A Wake-up Call

As I continued in the downward, spiritual spiral, things began to happen that jolted me out of my com-fort zone and helped me to wake up from my spiritual slumber - finally.

The moral integrity that existed in the group, the tremendous help and support system that was generated within it, together with the emotional bonds and fam-ily-like connections, had put a veil over my heart and mind. However, soon these aspects of my church started fading into the background and the dark clouds that hovered over my soul started to become apparent. These were dark clouds of subtle control and a toxic view of God. My reason and my intuition started to kick in but these would often give way to doubt. This was due to distorted interpretations of scripture, not taking into account context or history, and also because we were taught not to trust our feelings over and above

God's word. My church was not alone in what they be-lieved about God, Jesus, service, pastor's authority, etc. I had visited other churches, read books, heard Christian speakers and been a part of small Christian groups on my college campus. Most of them, more or less, echoed similar religious sentiments and doctrines. The Bible could not be wrong. It was Bible verses that had deeply touched my heart in my college room. So I allowed all interpretations of Bible passages by religious authorities, both inside and outside my church, to control my life. However, I continued to feel a stirring in my heart that made me restless. I just kept on thinking, "something is not right." I had forgotten that anyone's words could be twisted. God, unfortunately, was not exempt.

One incident that registered in my mind as a flag that something was amiss was when my 11-month old baby fell sick. That was the year when the winter was particularly harsh. My son had a fever for almost three weeks from a recurring ear infection that refused to go away, even after three rounds of antibiotics. Naturally, I did not take him to our early morning church service during that time. When he finally recovered and we brought him to our church Christmas party, I was chided because I kept my sick baby home instead of bringing him to "God's presence" in the church. I honestly did not see a point to spreading the virus that my son had, to other kids in the church. Could God be that legalistic about church attendance? Something snapped within me in that moment. I could not bring myself to believe that God could be that demanding. I chose to ignore it for the moment because I had enough "spiritual stress" to deal with, but once again my soul was disturbed. Something was not right.

The final wake-up call happened in the late spring of 2009. My sister had visited that past fall in 2008. She had professed her faith as a Christian many years prior and had then ventured to become an agnostic. She had backslidden. My pastor believed that God wanted him to pray over my sister for deliverance. My sister refused. She did not believe in any God at that point in her life, let alone Jesus. We were warned of God's disapproval and spiritual disaster for my sister's life. This did not help my already spiritually distressed state. However, to my utmost amazement, my sister called in the spring of the following year, just a few months after her visit, to tell us how she had been going through a hard time and had opened up the Bible (which my husband had given her) and it spoke loud and clear for her situation. She found a local church to worship in and continued to grow in faith. She began to hear God's voice like I had heard in my college days and my own drifting away from God became clearer to me. Now I wanted what she had. Additionally, there was another fact that I needed to deal with. God had reached out to my sister without the pastor's help. It hit me then that the man of God was only a man after all. My blind faith in my pastor took a hard hit that day.

The spiritual conflict I was experiencing further deepened. I knew I was right. Right about the fact that everything I was hearing in church about God and about the Bible was not a hundred percent accurate. But alas, I could not prove it to myself beyond shadows of doubt. This caused confusion. Moreover, I could not discuss this with any of my church friends or leaders. Any expression of conflict would mean that I was in "the devil's grip". Bringing up any of my spiritual struggles was going to be futile.

We were taught that any confusion was not of God. Sadly I believed that too. So I suffered in guilt because of experiencing such confusion.

I did not know then that my confusion was the beginning of God's great plan to deliver me from the shackles of religion.

eighteen

I Want Out

I had woken up to the shocking truth that my life was defined by karma consciousness (a performance-driven life) and Idolatry (idols of man and ministry, not stone and wood). I had been living under the illusion that upon becoming a Christian, I had been set free from "religion, into a relationship with God". I was shattered by the realization that, in fact, as a Christian, I had sunk deeper into religion. You can imagine my disappointment. Somewhere deep inside me, I wished to be free of the religious burden and have a relationship with God like I had always craved for, but there was a problem. My soul was already attached to a God I could not trust. At this point in time, my mind had been heavily conditioned by scriptures, for over 17 years, to fear and serve God. Yes He loved us but with a "tough love". I was always walking on egg-shells around Him, not knowing when He would be pleased and when He would turn on me.

Gradually, I started withdrawing from church. My health issues alone were enough to cause my dwindling attendance, but in fact, I was really burnt out by the very thought of God. I also could not endure sitting through another sermon or Bible study about how God "fought against His people". I also did not have the same zeal for praying with my pastor about my problems as I had been used to. My blind trust in him being God's representative for my life, had been shattered. I was disillusioned and needed some space in order to heal.

Last but not least, I wanted to withdraw from God. I was really exhausted having tried so hard to have a relationship with Him and failed. I noticed that some nonreligious people with whom I was acquainted had much more joy and peace in their lives than I ever did. It seemed like the only way for me to keep myself from having a complete physical, emotional and mental breakdown was to take a sabbatical from all things associated with God and church. However, I felt guilty because of the fact that God had healed me.

What if I left the church and hurt the pastor and the people, would I risk God's judgment? However, there was another thought that my newly awakened reason-ing latched onto: If atheists can be blessed by God, surely there is a ray of hope for me that God would leave me alone and let me live my life without Him. Yes, I was ready to take any risk. Everything to do with God had brought me stress and turmoil. I needed to get my life and health back. This meant leaving Christianity, leaving the USA and going back to my family, my roots in India and starting from scratch.

I badly wanted out.

While I made my exit (from Christianity) plans, Jesus was busy planning His entry (into my life).

AND THEN THERE WAS JESUS

The Spirit of the Sovereign LORD is on me because the LORD has anointed me to preach good news to the poor. He has sent me to bind up the brokenhearted, to proclaim freedom for the captives and release from darkness for the prisoners, to proclaim the year of the LORD's favor and the day of vengeance of our God, to comfort all who mourn, and provide for those who grieve in Zion - to bestow on them a crown of beauty instead of ashes, the oil of gladness instead of mourning, and a garment of praise instead of a spirit of despair. – Jesus (Isaiah 61:1-3, Luke 4:18-19)

"Come to me, all who are weary and heavy-laden, and I will give you rest. Take My yoke upon you and learn from me, for I am gentle and humble in heart, and you will find rest for your souls." – Jesus (Mathew 11:28-29)

Love Lifted Me

My husband had been very supportive throughout this time. He had been quick to recognize the spiritual pitfalls right from the start (if only I had done a better job of listening to him) but had been very patient with my need for my church family. He knew how much I missed my family in India and how much my church people meant to me. However, since early 2009, just when I started withdrawing emotionally from church, my husband also started feeling like our time there was up. He felt deep within that it was time to move on. This was not an easy decision to make. Church was the only family we knew away from home. It was the only family our children knew. We could not consider uprooting them. Also, I did not want to create any conflict and hurt feelings so I decided that the best way to leave would be to go back home to our families in India. That way, we could maintain good relations with all in the church and our children would not be deprived of family. Moreover, it would give me the space I needed, away from God and all religions, to rebuild my life. But alas, one cannot transport one's family across the ocean without a source of income. There was no job in sight in India. So we stayed on in the US and continued to go to church.

Another year went by.

It was the spring of 2010. I had come home from church discouraged and depressed again. This had now become the norm. I felt disappointed and heart-broken. I was grappling with the greatest betrayal of all: Christianity had failed me. It failed to bring me the inner strength and peace that I had hoped for. Listening to anything negative about God, in church, was not help-ing. Things which we had shared with our church leadership, such as reasons why we could not make it to church sometimes, were thrown back at us in the form of godly rebukes from behind the pulpit. This did not help either.

I remember that day very well. I had burst into tears during the church service. I was not able to stop crying even after coming home. All the emotions I had been holding in for several months burst forth. I cried out to God with all my strength. A deep ache went through my soul. 37 years of my life…..wasted! Wasted in serving a God who did not care, and who was punitive and harsh. I had set out to seek God in my childhood with innocent expectations of love and mercy and the hope of having Him as my friend. That did not happen. What did I get for my efforts? Sickness, guilt, fear and distress. I certainly did not get peace.

I remember being in a fetal position on the floor in my closet (I needed a private place to cry alone), unable to get a hold of my emotions. I was without God once more. I could not hear from Him, I could not trust Him. However, no matter how terrorized I felt by His judgments, there was still a little voice inside that wanted me to believe that He is good. I was confused, sad, feel-ing hopeless and kept on weeping uncontrollably.

I don't know what came over me but in that moment when I was breaking down, confused about Jesus, His character that is, something happened.

He touched me.

While I was crying out to Jesus, gentle waves of elec-tric-like currents went through my lower back and my legs and an ocean of love engulfed me. I felt a warm presence come over me. A tremendous peace engulfed my heart and mind. I burst forth speaking out in a language that I had never heard. I did not know what I was saying but it felt so beautiful and peaceful. As I continued to speak this unknown language an overwhelming sense of assurance came over me. I had stopped crying - like the still after a raging storm. Jesus had touched me and literally zapped (all puns intended) away the torment from within my soul. My Christian indoctrination had taught me that the only valid experience with God was either an interaction with the Bible or any-thing that the church leaders validated. These experiences were technically neither. All I knew was that pain had been plucked out from my heart. I had no idea what was happening to me but for the first time, in a long time, I felt a sense of stillness. My experience can best be described in the words of an old hymn:

"I was sinking deep in sin, far from the peaceful shore; Very deeply stained within sinking to rise no more; Then the master of the sea, heard my despairing cry; from the waters lifted me, now safe am I. Love lifted me, when nothing else could help love lifted me." (James Rowe, 1912)

In that moment in my closet, I learned three things about Jesus: that He is good, that He is love and that He cares.

My days as a "Christian" were over.

My journey with Jesus was about to begin.

twenty

New Wine, Old Wineskin

Jesus had touched me. I could finally be content in knowing that "God is love." (1 John 4:8) I could simply go back to my church life and continue status-quo. Problem solved. Right? Wrong. Although Jesus had touched me and awakened my spirit, my soul would be a long while catching up. The painful process of cleans-ing my soul from unhealthy attachments to people and mindsets, that had not only kept me from fully experiencing God's love but had also kept me from knowing Jesus true nature, was about to begin.

In the days and months that followed, I experienced everything I was taught to mistrust. Every experience was a miraculous manifestation of God's presence. Anytime I would say the name of Jesus, gentle currents and heat would go through my legs and the new, unknown prayer language (Acts 2:4) would pour out of my mouth. There were other times that I would be acutely aware of a presence by my side accompanied by the feeling of warmth all over me. My heart would be filled with peace. I felt a new and different desire for the Bible – thus far, I had been avoiding it due to the negative interpretations of many of its verses. Another time, I felt like someone was pouring warm honey over my ears, while I was searching the scriptures. Being able to connect positively with the Bible was a miracle. However, the greatest miracle of all was the fact that the very thought of Jesus was filling my heart with pleasure and warmth. I wanted to sing out loud and worship Him in the privacy of my home. I wanted to shout out His love with exuberance. Was I really the same person who had wanted to remove herself far, far away from God and Jesus?

Sadly, I felt like I needed to hide all these experiences from my church leaders and church people. I did not hope to have their validation for these experiences which were not based on the "word of God". We were taught not to trust our feelings and instincts over and above what the Bible said (interpretations acceptable to the leaders) The Holy Spirit's (Spirit of Jesus) gift of speaking in tongues (that is what I was experiencing) was acknowledged but not encouraged. When I was skeptical of this experience myself, why should I expect support from others? At first I also treated every experience that I had with caution, and tried to push it away, but the supernatural presence of Jesus was too powerful to ignore. No matter whether my experiences were "Biblically right or wrong", I could do nothing to stop them. As the days went by, the frequency of these experiences only increased. I could make no sense of anything that was happening to me. I only knew one thing. I was finally at peace – peace with God that is. Where my church life was concerned, I had no peace.

Jesus' presence in my private moments was very re-freshing for my heart. However, every time I went to church, I found myself slipping into the same toxic thought patterns and negative views of God. A civil war broke out in my soul. I had been disillusioned before but this was different. I felt my heart tear apart. If I did not go to church, I would lose all the relationships that I had invested in for over almost eighteen years (this is now early 2011). I ran the risk of breaking my pastor's heart and letting him down (remember I felt like I owed him my life and he took parental pride in me as an obedient daughter). What about the moral and spiritual foundation for my children? We had no replacement for our church family. However, the stark contrast between the Jesus I was experiencing outside of church and the one inside the church was causing me to lose my peace with God again – something I could not afford.

Yet, I would not leave. Soul ties are not easy to sever. The longer I stayed on, the worse things got.

We could not be involved to the same extent as before. We went from being "star" Christians to being "nonspiritual" and having a "rebellious" attitude. Even my husband was treated differently than what he was used to. Up until this point, he had been highly commended for his commitment and for serving in the church as both deacon and treasurer, but now things had changed. Perhaps our emotional withdrawal had caused misunderstandings which triggered the cold war. Nonetheless, relationships started deteriorating while we were still there. I badly wanted everything to be all right, but for that I would have to come out in the open about all my experiences, face the judgment and disapproval of the leaders for straying away from sound doctrine. I felt stuck.

While I was going through this predicament, the pastor asked me one day, "Do you not consider me your shepherd anymore?" He had sensed that I had stopped approaching him frequently for my prayer needs like I used to. His words pierced my heart. Indeed, if I left the church, I would not have a pastor as a shepherd, nor anyone to even say our last rites if something happened (like I said before, I did not know how to replace a church or pastor of 18 years, overnight). I was in my kitchen, lost in such thoughts, when I was acutely aware of that same presence again (the one that I had been experiencing lately) and a gentle whisper crossed my heart, "I myself will be your shepherd". I felt reassured. I had forgotten the words with which Jesus had touched me, in 1993, when I had first encountered a gentle but firm conviction from the Bible, "My sheep hear my voice…they follow me…they will not follow another." (1 John 10). This comforted me greatly. Although, I knew I would never be alone with Jesus by my side, I still chose to stay with my church. Some-times, it is very difficult, if not impossible, to break out of the status-quo.

It was the Easter of 2011. Our church service was outdoors. I was staring at a huge tree, towering big and tall, casting a huge shadow. I realized that no saplings or grass could grow in a healthy manner underneath that tree, for it was in the way, between them and the sun. All of a sudden, I had a moment, an epiphany if you will. I had to get out from under my church's shadow in order to continue to grow in the warmth of Jesus' love. Jesus' words rang true, "And no one puts new wine into old wineskins; otherwise the new wine will burst the skins and it will be spilled out, and the skins will be ruined. But new wine must be put into fresh wineskins." (Luke 5: 37-38) I could not ignore His gentle nudges anymore.

There was no second guessing. I needed to exit the environment which was causing me to suppress the new life within me.

I had to preserve the new wine, the old wineskin had to go.

twenty-one

Losing My World, Gaining My Soul

The old wineskin had to go. God had impressed this upon my heart in many different ways, but I could not gather the courage to let it go.

Our church started a Bible study series on how God's people were judged for their "ever complaining" attitude. The introductory video for this series left me speechless. The speaker, in the video, was all fired up about God's judgment of His very own children. The people in the passage being discussed had a long history of rejecting God's love. The context was not taken into account. The Jesus who touched me had been far from vindictive. I was deeply disturbed by the discrepancy between what I was experiencing and what I was learning. My soul was far from being nurtured. I felt disheartened. So I decided to stay away from these Bible studies. However, Jesus had his own plans to feed my soul.

One Sunday I woke up with a strong conviction

that I needed to go to a certain church that I had visited when I was in school. The name of the church flashed in my mind. I needed to obey this gentle and firm conviction so I went. Alone. It was a huge crowd, compared to the few in my church, and I noticed the free flow in worship right away. I felt healed within my soul and the service had not even started. Once the sermon began, I was stunned. It was as if Jesus had taken over the speaker and the entire message was just for me - me in a crowd of hundreds of people. Every word a healing balm and every pause the very breath of Jesus on me. My tears kept flowing. This is what I had been missing in my church experience. I could not remember the last time I had felt close to Jesus and His love in a church setting. I kept coming back for more. I was not disappointed. Every Sunday was the same experience. It felt like a dream. Could God really talk to me at such length and in such details through a speaker who did not even know that I existed? How is it that I felt so validated and healed in this church?

One night, during this time, I had a strange dream. I dreamt that I was reading the passage in the Bible where God had delivered His children from slavery to the nation of Egypt. In my dream I saw a part in the Bible where God tells His people not to go back to Egypt (the place of their bondage). I felt like that warning was for me. That God had touched me and delivered me from an unhealthy mindset…that I needed to not go back into that. For a true and complete deliverance I would need a different church. He had spoken to me in several days, but this dream convicted me deeply.

I found the courage I needed.

We wanted to leave with dignity and without hurting anyone's feelings. We wanted to make it clear that it was not about rejecting the fellowship of the people whom we cared about, but about our very relationship with God that needed a different space to grow. However, the misunderstandings caused by our lack of attendance took precedence over any other issue we may have tried to discuss. I expected to be labelled un-spiritual and manipulated by the devil (when I tried to explain my spiritual experience in my closet, I was cautioned against the devil's tricks, for he can masquerade as an "angel of light"). However, I was not prepared for the shocking accusations and pronouncements of God's judgment and wrath on us. We were warned of spiritual disaster for our children, once they were uprooted. We were also warned about the inevitable judgment of God for having hurt His ministry in the church. After all the years of loyalty, especially from my husband who had, many times, taken a stand for the pastor against dis-gruntled church members, we did not expect to be accused of hurting the very mission and people that we poured ourselves into. My husband was confronted re-garding his "betrayal of

Jesus" because he was a deacon and on leaving the church, he would be leaving that ministry as well. I was accused of boycotting church activities by influencing my friends not to attend. This accusation left me speechless. That my church leaders, the ones who had praised me endlessly for my service in the church, should believe that I was capable of creating factions in the church, shattered me completely.

We wanted to leave with as much as honor as we could. However, we found ourselves in an emotional battle of accusations and guilt, something we were com-pletely unprepared for. My world fell apart. Not because I was leaving my church family, but because both mine and my husband's characters were run to the ground in the name of holy confrontation and tough love. All this while, my church leadership believed that they were fulfilling their responsibilities and duties towards God.

I understood the power of religion that day.

We had hoped to leave the church on cordial terms with everyone. We had hoped to clear our misunderstandings, explain our reason to leave as purely God-led (which it was and which, when we tried to explain, we were warned not to take God's name in vain) and move on with mutual agreement, having reconciled our differences. However, the only reconciliation acceptable was that we repent and go back to doing the things we used to do. It was too late for that. I had tasted the love of Jesus.

There was no turning back.

I had never expected to ever leave my church. I imagined that if I ever left, perhaps due to moving out of the city, that I would leave with dignity. I left with ac-cusations, rejection and tears.

We lost everything that day. It wasn't just the phys-ical loss of family ties. Our characters had been questioned. I was used to living with praises. Now I would have to live with reproach. We would not be re-membered well in the hearts of the very people we served with our life. We also lost trust in human relationships that day. We were about to step into an emotional and social vacuum.

Jesus' words hit home, "What good will it be for someone to gain the whole world, yet forfeit their soul? Or what can anyone give in exchange for their soul?" (Mathew 16:26)

On June 19, 2011 I forfeited my world (my church). I hoped to gain my soul.

twenty-two

Father Forgive Them

Which comes first? Healing or forgiveness? Both go hand in hand. Without forgiveness there can be no healing and without healing it is difficult to forgive.

The Christian is not given a choice. Jesus, himself, set the example, "Father forgive them for they (the peo-ple who put Him on the cross and ill-treated Him) know not what they do." (Luke 23:34)

I had set out to gain my soul but I found myself in a pit of grief, anger, bitterness, regrets, pain and, of course, unforgiveness. One thing was certain. There would be no gaining of my soul without healing. The healing could not be complete without forgiveness. So I set out to forgive; but no matter how hard I tried, I found a deep ache inside my soul and the feelings of hurt resulting in bitterness surfaced time and again. Forgiveness seemed impossible...but wait a minute. Is anything impossible for God? Indeed it was Jesus' presence and guidance throughout the process that helped me both forgive and heal. I have to describe some of those miraculous moments, when He reached out to me over and over again.

It was not just people that I needed to forgive. I needed to forgive myself. I felt deep regret for the time that I had wasted letting my life revolve around a group for so long. I felt like I was responsible for getting my husband and myself both into a state of ill health due to the stress in our lives. Forgiving others is sometimes easier than forgiving one's self. We cannot do it without the Lord's touch. I remember that day when my husband was traveling. I was alone with Jesus and with my heartaches and regrets, asking Him the classic question, "Why?" Jesus chose not to answer me. He answered my husband instead. My husband who had fallen asleep on his flight, was awakened and he felt that the words of Jesus (to Peter) were impressed upon his heart - "Si-mon, Simon, Satan has asked to sift all of you as wheat. But I have prayed for you, Simon that your faith may not fail. And when you have turned back, strengthen your brothers." (Luke 22:31-32). As my husband shared that incident with me, I was deeply moved, indeed I was not the victim of my choices. God had a good plan for all that we had been through. I needed to let go of hold-ing myself responsible. The healing began.

One other time, when I was at the grocery store,

an elderly woman walked up to me and handed me a piece of paper with her testimony typed up on it. I read it in the parking lot and went back inside to thank her. She just looked at me and said, "it's people isn't it? It's always people, we hurt each other and cause pain." She assured me that Jesus can change hearts and that I needed to stand firm in forgiveness. It was just what I needed to hear that day. I had only one question for her, how did she know?

As Jesus kept cheering me on this journey of forgiveness and healing, an incident at church impacted me deeply. I was at this new church. I had resolved not to get involved or let people even know my name there. I was starting over and this time I did not want to be distracted from Jesus. Getting involved with the people and the activities prematurely would only set me up to fall into similar temptations as before. That day, a guest speaker had spoken and the message touched me deeply. When the altar was opened up for prayer (this was a practice I was not accustomed to in a church set-ting) I went forward and kneeled down and quietly prayed by myself. While my eyes were still closed, I felt a touch on my shoulder. A lady from the church had gotten out of her seat, knelt down beside me and offered to pray for me. The words that came out of her mouth made me jump out of my skin. She assured me that Jesus was there when I had been accused and that He knew my pain and how much I was wounded inside by people whom I was very close to. She further went on to reassure me that God had a plan for me and that He wanted me to give up my offense to Him. I was overcome with emotions. She prayed and left. She did not even ask for my name. Was this an angel? No, I saw her in church randomly many times after that. She was only human, operating in the Holy Spirit's gift of prophecy, one of the manifestations of the spirit of Jesus. Jesus had not only acknowledged my pain but had directly commanded me to let it go. Nothing else could have brought me the inner healing I felt that day.

As the days went by and Jesus helped further my un-derstanding of His love, I understood forgiveness better. He showed me that the people who had offended me were just as much in need of His love and touch as I was. He did not judge them, He did not judge me. He loved them. He loved me.

Letting go of the past is a process. The apostle Paul understood this when he said, "Brothers and sisters, I do not consider myself yet to have taken hold of it. But one thing I do: Forgetting what is behind and straining toward what is ahead, I press on toward the goal to win the prize for which God has called me heavenward in Christ Jesus." (Philippians 3:13-14)

I am so glad Jesus took hold of me. If not, where would I be?

twenty-three

A New Creation

Change is inevitable. Change is a process. Change does not happen overnight. Change is painful.

Very painful.

Following my exit from my church, I set out on a journey with Jesus. At first it looked like my whole life had fallen apart, everything destroyed. In fact, Jesus was reconstructing my life, I did not quite understand it then. This quote by Cynthia Occelli best captured my situation - "For a seed to achieve its greatest expression, it must come completely undone. The shell cracks, its insides come out and everything changes. To someone who doesn't understand growth, it would look like com-plete destruction." All I felt was pain then, but it was all worth it in the end.

While we were at the church, we did not have the time or opportunity to develop or nurture very many friendships outside the group. No wonder, when we left, we plunged into an emotional and social vacuum. I was so badly hurt that I lost trust in relationships and friendships and for the longest time, I would not open myself to making any new friends - especially not at church. I sank into depression and stayed there for quite some time. I had always been a "people's person", I didn't know what to do. But Jesus was not going to let me go into that lonely place. It had been four years now since we left. I look around and I see people. Friendships that blossomed out of the blue. It would take another book to describe the beautiful manner in which Jesus healed my heart, provided good friends and kindred spirits to spur me on my life's journey.

Many-a-time when people leave a ministry or religious group, they undergo fear and guilt if they do so without the leader's approval. They live with a vague sense of fear that they have somehow lost God's favor and protection. This is not unique to any one religion. I have experienced this in both religions that I have been through. Often, when members leave without the leader's consent, because they have hurt the "man of God" they are warned of God's judgment. I had tasted Jesus' love but letting go of unhealthy views of God would take time. Although I knew that I had left my church with deep conviction from God, I still felt guilt for having caused any inadvertent pain to all the people who cared for me and I for them. So when at first, things seemed to go out of control, it was very natural for me to think that God was perhaps displeased with me. However, the warmth of Jesus' presence and His assurance, "Never will I leave you, never will I forsake you", sustained me. Never means never. Jesus is no liar.

I learned not to interpret good or bad events in my life as whether or not I have God's love and favor. I was about to learn the greatest lesson of my life in the years to come-no matter what happens in our life, good or bad, Jesus loves us. The apostle Paul bears witness to that, "It is God who justifies. Who is to condemn? Christ Jesus is the one who died — more than that, who was raised — who is at the right hand of God, who indeed is interceding for us. No, in all these things we are more than conquerors through him who loved us. For I am sure that neither death nor life, nor angels nor rulers, nor things present nor things to come, nor powers, nor height nor depth, nor anything else in all creation, will be able to separate us from the love of God in Christ Je-sus our Lord." (Romans 8:34-39).

One day, I woke up and I got that. The above passage from the Bible, became real. I was (am) loved. It was (is) all about His presence, not my performance.

Four years have passed since I held His hand and jumped. I had jumped into what seemed like a pit of de-pression and loneliness and uncertainty. However, it was also the time when I experienced

His presence and miraculous touch in my life like never before. In fact, I had not jumped into a pit but onto a rock- a Rock (Jesus) that is more than able to sustain me. My health improved greatly. He provided me with a new career, new friends, new life and a new spirit and even a new God a new way of relating to Jesus. Nobody has a perfect life here on earth. I won't either. Thank God, Jesus holds my hand. That is my one and only hope.

"Therefore if anyone is in Christ, He is a new creation. Behold, all old things have passed away, all things have become new." (2 Corinthians 5:17)

Becoming new is not a magical event. The old must go.

Actually, the old must be annihilated.

twenty-four

In Retrospect

Hindsight is 20/20 – always.

I had witnessed Jesus' power in my life. This made me cross over from Hinduism to Christianity. It was natural for me to want to learn from those who had helped save my life and inspire me spiritually. At first, I needed to rely on other people's experiences with Christ and Christianity. I was from a different religious back-ground, after all. However, I made the mistake of believing that I could not know Jesus like the leaders who were in ministry and so I let them define God's purposes for my life. But when life, itself came at me, I found that I could not stand. No one has described my situation better than Jesus Himself. Listen to His words, "Therefore everyone who hears these words of mine and puts them into practice is like a wise man who built his house on the rock. The rain came down, the streams rose, and the winds blew and beat against that house; yet it did not fall, because it had its foundation on the rock. But everyone who hears these words of mine and does not put them into practice is like a foolish man who built his house on sand. The rain came down, the streams rose, and the winds blew and beat against that house, and it fell with a great crash." (Mathew 7:24-27). I had not taken the time to grow or nurture my personal experiences with Jesus. No wonder my spiritual house fell with a great crash.

Since then, I have learned that spiritual growth cannot be measured by our church attendance or moral standing. It cannot be measured by the favor we have with our church leaders. I was under the illusion that I must appear with my spiritual achievements before God in order to be acceptable to Him. Nothing could have been further from the truth. All I had needed to do all along, was to embrace Jesus' righteousness (which He imparted to me through His sacrifice) as my own. This was His gift to me. I had to reach out with faith and accept that gift - that's what I should have done. I thought believing in Christ's divinity and serving in church was enough, gaining the leaders' approval and seeking after God's will was all that I needed to do to earn God's favor. However, eventually I did learn this lesson: that I cannot earn God's love and favor. They are already mine through Jesus. By far, the most im-portant lesson I learned is that Jesus has not left us alone. His Holy Spirit manifests powerfully in us, pouring His love into our hearts and endowing us with gifts (supernatural manifestations) to bring healing and hope to those who will receive it.

Hindsight is indeed 20/20.

My supernatural experiences (more than what I have written about) have not made me a super human in any way. There are good days. There are bad days. My spiritual experiences with Jesus have, in fact, made me more human. I am now more in touch with my human self than ever before. It is a truly humbling yet liberating experience to celebrate my humanness before God. His mercy sustains me. My journey with Jesus has only begun. I must renew my vision of Jesus every day even as He reaches out to me with the spirit of love, warmth, compassion and through the Bible that comes alive in fresh ways, not as a rule book but as a love letter from my Creator. Intimacy with Jesus is now the most important aspect of my Christian life. I cannot allow myself to carry the heavy yoke that religious traditions demand. I would rather carry the yoke that Jesus gives. Listen to His words of compassion, "Come to me, all you who are weary and burdened, and I will give you rest. Take my yoke upon you and learn from me, for I am gentle and humble in heart, and you will find rest for your souls. For my yoke is easy and my burden is light." (Mathew 11:28-30) His burden is light.

The emotional connections I had with my

church family will always remain in some corner of my heart. Many Christmases have been celebrated with them. Sadly, I was unable to fit into their spiritual structure. My longing for God since my childhood days would not let me be content in that structure. No amount of any religious discipline can replace Jesus. That's all.

I am certainly no authority where Christianity is concerned. It is a vast religion with many denominations and aspects. I can only speak from my personal experience – behavior modification and good moral standing and church disciplines are simply not enough. Christianity minus Christ, specifically the love of Christ, just does not work. Only a heart touched by the love of Jesus can be at peace. Only a heart transformed by the love of Jesus can grow spiritually - grow into being more like Him.

Christianity is not about us and how good we can be. It's about Him.

There is no one like Jesus. No one.

twenty-five

I Love To Tell The Story

Not in my wildest imagination, did it ever occur to me that my journey with God that began with temple bells, would end in Jesus. The journey has been a spiritual roller coaster. It has not been easy for me to expose my spiritual struggles. The hardest part of writing this book has been writing about my struggles in church. However, I needed to share my story for there are many Christians who need to hear the two things I needed to hear most about Jesus: that He is good and that He cares.

I shared my story with the hope of prompting a fresh look at Jesus, who He was, and what He came to do. He came to give us life - eternal life, abundant life. In his own words, "The thief comes only to steal and kill and destroy; I came that they may have life, and have it abundantly." (John 10:10). "I am the resurrection and the life, He who believes in me, will live, even if he dies." (John 11:25). Jesus' character and mission (to bring God's gift of salvation, to heal the broken hearted, to comfort those who grieve –Isaiah 61) can sometimes get lost in church socials, church traditions and in a harsh, demanding, and punitive view of God. Many religious leaders seem to be afraid to focus on God's love because of the belief that it will give people the "license to sin." In fact, it is His love that heals and transforms us.

I shared my story to encourage those who may have been disappointed or disillusioned by their church experience like I was. I needed time to heal. If I had not tasted the loving kindness of Jesus, I would not have gone back to church. Being part of a church family is a blessing. It is a blessing to be able to express our heartfelt worship to Jesus together with other people of faith. A local church body works as a team to spread the love and goodness of Jesus to those in need. However, a church is made of people. Imperfect people, like you and me. Sometimes things go wrong. Our hearts break. Since we can often not separate God and church (in our minds they are one entity), we give up on both. I know, I did. Sharing my story is my attempt to tell you that there is a God and he cares for you very, very much. Allow Him to heal that wound. Allow Him to enter in-side your heart and fill the cracks.

Yes, church is a good thing. Religious control is not. If religious control supersedes our church experience, then we will surely lose sight of the very one for whom and by whom the church exists. Church leaders carry a tremendous responsibility on their shoulders. They need our prayers and support. However, there is a dangerous trend in many Christian groups of replacing Jesus with "anointed leaders." Pastor, Author and Director of Foundation Ministries, Mike Fehlauer, has this to say, "When we pursue the honor of men, we do so at the expense of our relationship with God. If we continue to do so, gradually men will take the place of God in our lives. An unhealthy soul tie is created, and our sense of confidence is determined by our standing with those in leadership. This kind of control will destroy people spiritually!" (Excerpt from his article, Warning Signs of Spiritual Abuse, on CBN.com).

My experiences caused me to step back and ask a deeper question? Who am I? Is my identity defined by my religion? Am I a Hindu? A Jain? A Christian? If a Christian, then am I Baptist, Evangelical, Pentecostal or nondenominational? Should it matter? Why can't I be defined as a wonderfully crafted masterpiece (Ephe-sians 2:10) of an amazing creator who knit me together in my mother's womb (Psalm 139:13) and loved me with an everlasting love? (Jeremiah 31:3) Jesus said, "Greater love has no man than this, that a man should lay down his life for his friends" (John 15:13). This makes me God's friend - an identity Jesus died to give me...

And you.

The day I left my church, I felt like I had lost my pur-pose in life. I have regained my purpose since then. It is to tell the story of Jesus and His love, as described in this old hymn by Katherine Hankey (1834-1911) –

"I love to tell the story;
more wonderful it seems
than all the golden fancies
of all our golden dreams.
I love to tell the story,
it did so much for me;
and that is just the reason
I tell it now to thee.

Refrain:
I love to tell the story,
'twill be my theme in glory,
to tell the old, old story
of Jesus and his love."

"May you experience the love of Christ, though it is too great to understand fully. Then you will be made complete with all the fullness of life and power that comes from God." (Ephesians 3:19, NLT Bible)

ABOUT THE AUTHOR

Pooja Chilukuri resides in the Raleigh-Durham area of North Carolina where she is a certified health coach with a passion for wellness education. Her greatest passion, however, is to tell the story of Jesus' love, which she shares in her first book, a memoir entitled, And Then There Was Jesus. Pooja's hobbies include reading, writing, and enjoying life with her family and friends.

Print copies of this book can be purchased from Rain Publishing and online bookstores.
www.rainpublishing.com

You can also mail your request to:

Please include the following with your order: Title, number of copies, shipping address, contact information, payment ($11.99 x # of copies) including shipping ($5.00), and mail to:

Pooja Chilukuri/Rain Publishing PO Box 702 Knightdale, NC 27545